OPTIONS TRADING

HOW TO MAKE PROFIT FOR A LIVING AND GENERATE A PASSIVE INCOME WORKING FROM HOME

ROBERT EATON

COPYRIGHT

© Copyright 2021 by Robert Eaton

All rights reserved.

CONTENTS

INTRODUCTION

There are many skills that can help you be a successful trader in the world of options trading. It also consists of the ability to evaluate the company fundamentals and to determine the direction of a stock trend. But, apart from all these, there is one more important skill. It is the psychology of the trader. Having emotion, think quickly, and exercising discipline are some of the main components of what is being collectively known as trading psychology. While talking about emotions, there are two types of emotions that you will need to keep under control—fear and greed.

- **Understanding Fear**

Whenever a trader gets to know something bad about a stock or about the complete economy, he/she will have a tendency to feel scared. That is completely normal. The trader might start overreacting as well. He might think of liquidating all his holdings and sit on the cash. The trader might feel scared about making any other trade.

When you enter the world of trading, you are needed to have a clear understanding of what fear exactly is. It is a natural form of reaction that gets perceived to any kind of threat. In this case, the threat is meant for the potential nature of profits. When you start quantifying all your fears, it might help. You are required to find the root of your fear and find the reason behind it. But, this form of thinking needs to appear before any bad news comes up and not after something bad has happened. When you think about it properly, by taking some time, you will be able to gain knowledge about how you perceive various small events. You will come to know the way you react to them. This will help you greatly to maintain a distance from your emotional responses. This whole thing might not feel that easy. But it is very important for the perfect health of your trading portfolio.

- **Opting or Research and Review**

You need to be an expert in the stocks and industries that you find interest in. try your best to be updated with the market news, keep on educating yourself, and just keep your eyes open. If you get the opportunity of attending trading seminars, just go for them. You are required to dedicate most of your time to the research process. You will need to speak up with the trading management, study the data charts, read trading journals, and opt for background jobs, such as analysis of the industry. As you continue reviewing and researching, you can gain more ideas about options trading. You can overcome the darkness of fear with this.

- **Speedy Decisions**

Traders are required to think quickly and make super-fast decisions at times. You being a trader, might need to sell out and buy stocks on a very short time notice as well. In order to accomplish all these, you will need to maintain a particular presence in your mind. You need to be disciplined to stick to your own plans of action. You are required to know the perfect time for generating profits and incurring losses. There is no way in which you can permit your emotions to come in the way of decision-making.

- **Fighting Greed**

'Pigs get slaughtered' is a very common saying on Wall Street. This indicates the greedy habit of the traders by sticking to one position for winning for a very long time. It is done to get each and every penny from the rise of the stock price. Well, in the near future, the same stock will tend to take a reverse turn, and you, as a greedy investor, will get trapped. Greed is not at all an easy thing to fight with. It is completely based on the instincts of human beings to do even better. It is the habit of gaining a little more than what you are currently having. It involves the sense of being unsatisfied. If you want to be successful in the world of trading, you will need to identify this instinct of yours. You will need to set a plan which will be based on your rational way of thoughts, accompanied by no forms of whims or instincts.

- **Setting Rules**

A trader must design new rules every day and follow them whenever the hit of psychology comes into the picture. You can start by setting out various forms of guidelines based on your risk-award tolerance when you make any trade. You will need to ensure your profit target from trade and employ stop loss for moving away from all your emotions from its way. You can also determine the types of events, positive or negative, that will be triggering the decisions related to selling or buying any stock. It would be good for you if you could just out certainly limit to the maximum amount that you will be profiting or losing in one day. After you have touched your decided mark, take out all your money, and just run. If the loss target has already been hit by a trade, it would be better for you to pack up your bags and return back home.

Either of the two ways, you will be able to live for trading on the next day. If you try to move away from the limits, the time is near when you will be losing all that you have, with no chance of trading in the near future. Trading is a risky affair, my friend. You need to look out for the perfect conditions and also identify your limits for making the best out of it.

- **Being Flexible**

You need to be flexible as being an investor. You will need to find out some time to experiment at fixed intervals. For example, you might think of investing in options to mitigate all your risks. The only way by which you can grab all the knowledge about the market of trading is by experimenting. The experience that you will be gaining from the events can assist you in controlling your emotions. You will need to assess your own performance. As you review your trading performances, it can help in reflecting on how you have prepared yourself for the new trading session. You need to be updated about each and every condition of the market, so that you can modify your plans according to the condition. Being flexible is the key to successful trading, as if you try to be confined within your fixed plans, there are chances that you will lose. This is mainly because of the volatile nature of the trading market.

OPTIONS TRADING: THE BASICS

There are a lot of terms and language a novice options trader needs to learn before beginning to invest. You'll learn about them here, as well as gaining more insight into what they are about.

Let's start with the basic vocabulary.

Learning the Lingo

- Writer: this is the individual offering the options contract.
- Volatility: refers to the frequency and degree of movement an asset's price can take. Some assets offer high volatility (frequent and large price swings), some don't. Low volatility assets tend to be considered more appropriate for conservative portfolios, while high volatility assets tend to be more appropriate for aggressive portfolios.
- Hedging: is a method used to reduce investment risk. Using "married" or "covered" (not the same thing), options where the writer owns the assets the options are written for, can protect the asset owner from volatility.
- Beta: this is a measure of an asset's volatility compared to that of other securities in the same market.

- We also have language for the actual options themselves. These terms describe whether the option is for buying or selling the asset and the prices involved. The challenge is that traders often use a variety of synonyms for these basic terms.
- Calls (Call options): the option writer uses these to give the buyer the ability to buy an asset when it reaches a specific price.
- Puts (Put options): the option writer uses these to give the buyer the ability to sell an asset when it reaches a specified price.
- Expiration: options contracts are written for a specific period of time. This can range from a few days, all the way to a few years or longer. As you might expect, the longer the contract, the higher the price the option buyer will pay.
- Premium: this is the price the buyer pays for the options.
- Employee Stock Option: Higher-ranking company employees often receive stock options as part of their compensation. These options grant the recipient the right to buy a specific number of shares at a fixed price. If the company's stock value goes up, the employee can exercise the stock option to benefit from the increase. If the company stock fails to rise in value, the employee doesn't make any money off the option. The idea is that the options are only worth something if the company's value is increased, motivating the employees to do their best.
- Contract size: generally, 100 shares when buying or selling an option on a particular stock. The price of the option will be given per share. For example: a $2 option for 100 shares would cost $200.
- Options traders also have terms they use to describe where the option is in its life. These terms refer to the "moneyness" of the option.
- In the money: the asset has achieved the required price movement to reward the buyer.
- Out of the money: the asset has not achieved the price necessary to reward the option buyer.

- At the money: the asset is at a price necessary to activate the option terms for the buyer.
- Investors also have terms to specify their market approach and evaluation. These terms indicate whether a trader is optimistic or pessimistic about the particular market.
- Bulls, bullish: plays off the idea that bulls are aggressive animals that charge forward. A "bullish" trader is optimistic that the market prices are going to rise or continue to rise.
- Bears, bearish: plays on the idea of bears being lumbering animals that hibernate for long stretches of time. A "bearish" trader is pessimistic about the market's prospects. He or she may sit on the sidelines (not invest at all) or make investments to take advantage of the market downturn they anticipate.
- Going long: the trader is bullish on the market or a particular asset.
- Going short: the trader is bearish on the market or a particular asset. Not the same as "selling short," which will be explained in the paragraph on buying/selling language.
- Contrarian investor: some investors feel the best approach is to defy the prevailing opinion and invest in the opposite direction of everyone else.

Sometimes only part of an investment market will be rising while the rest of that market may be declining or falling when the rest of the market is rising. Since markets are made up of large numbers of companies/assets, it shouldn't be surprising that different parts are moving in different directions. One thing to remember is that you can make money no matter which direction the market is moving in.

There are a variety of terms traders use to describe their maneuvers. Let's look at them in the next paragraph on buying/selling language:

- Bid: the price a potential buyer is willing to pay for an asset
- Ask: the price a potential seller is willing to sell the asset for

- Bid/ask spread: this refers to the difference between the bid and asks prices.
- Selling short: this is a bearish technique that investors use when they expect the price of an asset to decline. The investor "borrows" the asset, usually from a broker, and then sells it at the current market price. If the asset price declines, the investor can then replace the borrowed asset with one that costs less than what the investor sold the original asset for. Of course, asset prices can rise as well as fall. If the asset in question goes up in price rather than down, the short seller must still replace the borrowed asset, but now must pay more for the replacement, thus losing money. Short sales can be quite risky because the best the short seller can do is double their money if the asset value declines to nothing, but an asset's price can increase with no limit.
- Uptick rule: short sales have been controversial at times. Often, investors blame short sales for market declines, even though every short sale guarantees future stock purchases (to replace the shorted shares). Uptick rules (if they exist for the asset you're following) prevent short sellers from shorting an asset unless its price has "ticked" upward.

Brokers, Brokerages, and Floor Brokers

Once you're ready to start trading, you're going to need to find someone to handle your transactions for you. This person or company is known as a broker, and there are several different types.

A "broker" is someone who acts as the middleman (woman) who handles buying and selling assets between investors. Brokers fall into two categories: full commission brokers and discount brokers. Here's a breakdown of each:

•Full Commission Broker: this is the traditional broker. They provide advice, handle paperwork, manage accounts (even buying and selling at their discretion depending on the broker/client relationship), and charge the "full" commission rate, which will vary depending on the size of your account.

•Discount Broker: these brokers discount their services and count on large numbers of clients to succeed. A discount broker won't offer specific advice (they may publish a newsletter or investment guide sent to all their clients), handle paperwork, or manage your account for you. This is fine for many of today's investors, who want to take charge of their investments rather than rely on a broker. Options traders usually prefer discount brokers to help keep their costs down. Traders do need to do their research before selecting a broker (something the next chapter covers) since extra fees can eat into your resources.

•Brokerage: a "brokerage," of "brokerage house," is simply a collection of brokers who are part of a company designed for investment management.

Options Types

There are two basic approaches to how options are created and managed. These are known as "American Style Options," and "European Style Options." While there are similarities between the two types, it's what they do differently, that's important here.

While you may think that they use European style in Europe and American style in the United States, that isn't the case. Instead, it varies from investment option to investment option.

Perhaps the most significant difference between the two is that holders of the American style can execute their option at any time before the expiration date. Holders of European style option do not. Obviously, this can be a big deal depending on the volatility of the investment.

Another difference is the two options styles expire on different days of the week. American style typically expires on the third Friday of the month the contract ends. European style options expire the third Thursday of the month the contract ends.

Generally, stocks and ETFs (Exchange Traded Funds, a type of open-ended fund that can be traded just like stocks) trade under the American style. With stock indices, most trade under the European option style (limited indices such as the S&P 100 are an exception).

Binary Options

These are a special type of option with only a put or call choice. They are very simple propositions of the "yes/no" variety. An example would be a binary option for the price of a stock being greater than $100 share by 4 p.m. You will have a choice of a bid or ask price, which is set by traders based on the perceived likelihood of one being more likely to win.

Binary options bid/ask prices will always be between $100 and $0. If traders feel the likelihood of one side or the other is close, you'll likely see a bid/ask of around $49/$51. If there's a great likelihood of the stock exceeding the target price by the deadline, then the bid/ask might be closer to $85/$87 or higher.

Let's say you paid $51 for your binary option, and the stock makes good. You'll receive the $100 value of the binary option. This gives you a profit of $49 minus commission or fees. You are "in the money." If the stock fails to beat the target price, then you're out the $51 plus commission or fees. You are "out of the money."

The bid and ask price will fluctuate depending on the stock price's movement before the deadline. Because they are so simple, binary options are popular choices for beginning investors and those without a lot of time to spend managing their money. You can purchase more than one binary option contract increasing your profit or loss potential.

Settlement Price Determination

Another difference between the two options styles is how and when the option settlement price is determined. The settlement price for American-style options is determined by the regular closing price of the asset at the end of the trading day, the third Friday of the month. Trades that occur after hours do not have any effect on this price. With European-style options, the settlement price usually isn't known until sometime during the next trading day.

Other Terms

- "Automatic" Exercise: your broker will exercise the expiring option to protect you.
- Auto Trading: you can make an agreement with your broker to automatically execute a position if certain market conditions are met.
- Open/Close: beginning and ending of the trading day. Also used to refer to a security's price at either point. For example: "Shares of ABC Corporation opened higher this morning (or closed lower this afternoon)."
- Correction: a stock price drop that quickly rebounds
- Decay/Time Decay: refers to the gradual reduction in the time left for the options contract.
- Dividend: companies reward stockholders in one of two ways. The price of the stock can increase, or the company can share profits with shareholders by paying them some of those profits per shares held by each stockholder. These payments are called dividends. Generally, the price of the stock declines by an

amount similar to the dividend, since the company is worthless after paying out that money. If you hold an option for a stock that pays out a dividend during the contract period, the value of that dividend has to be factored into the stock price.

- Fundamentals: some investors base their investment decisions on readily available information on a company's finances, assets, and other historical data. These include share price versus historical share price, price to earnings ratio [P/E], cash flow, return on assets, etc.
- Technical Analysis: these investors rely on analyzing the behavior of a stock or stocks and look for indicators they feel predict movement.

TECHNICAL ANALYSIS VS. FUNDAMENTAL ANALYSIS

What Is Technical Analysis?

If you want to fully understand and predict what the entry and exit points in the market should be, then understanding technical analysis should be your first and foremost priority. Fundamental analysis is all about making decisions based on industry trends, valuation, and revenue. On the other hand, technical analysis is about volume and price from historical data. In this method, investors implement behavioral economics and statistical analysis so that they can bridge the gap between market price and intrinsic value.

In technical analysis, there are two different approaches, and it is important that you choose the right one for yourself.

- Top-Down: This approach is more about macroeconomic analysis. This means that this approach is less about individual securities and more about the overall economy. The primary focus will be on the economy, and then the focus will shift to the various sectors and then finally to the companies present in those sectors.
- Bottom-Up: The next one is just the opposite, where the

investors focus more on individual stocks rather than a macroeconomic analysis. If a particular stock seems interesting, then this approach will help in finding the possible entry and exit points in that stock.

What Is Fundamental Analysis?

Now, let us move on to one of the cornerstones of the finance world, that is, fundamental analysis. If you want to predict the future price of underlying securities, then understanding fundamental analysis is very important. There are several components that are studied here to perform an in-depth analysis of the market and not only understand the economy but also the company and the industry in which it operates. Once you have this data in your hands, you will be able to predict the future of market developments and also know what value does the stock of a particular company has. You will also be able to find out if a particular stock is undervalued or overvalued. If you are able to perform the fundamental analysis perfectly, then you will also be able to point out investment opportunities that others have not yet noticed.

Some of the components of a stock that are analyzed are as follows, competitor analysis, external politics, trade agreements, news releases, global industry, political conditions within the country, press releases of the company, and financial statements of the company.

If there is a bad impact on any of these fundamental indicators, then there is a possibility that the share price will be negatively affected. Similarly, if there is a positive change in the indicators, the stock price of that particular company will be boosted.

How to Get Started with Technical Analysis?

If you are just a beginner, then here are some of the basic steps that you should implement in order to get started with technical analysis.

- Develop a trading system: This is the first step, and it means you have to identify a technical analysis strategy that works for you. For example, if you are a beginner, then you might go for the moving average crossover strategy. In this method, you will be keeping track of the two moving averages on any particular stock's changes in price.
- Find the right strategy for your tradable security: Not every strategy is meant for all securities. If your tradable securities are options, then you have to find the strategy that fits them. Sometimes, the parameter choices also start changing with the security you choose.
- Choose the right brokerage account: The next step is to choose the right brokerage account where you will be able to trade the type of security you have chosen. Not every brokerage account gives you the tools needed to perform technical analysis of options. The brokerage account you choose should have proper monitoring and tracking functionality with the technical indicators you need. Also, you need to make sure that your costs are low so that your profits are not affected.
- Choose an interface to monitor trades: Depending on the strategy you have chosen, the functionality you also need changes. So, choose your interface carefully.
- See whether you need any more applications: Sometimes, in order to maximize the performance, you might need other applications too. Some traders prefer trading on the go, and so they look for platforms that would give them mobile alerts. So, if there are any such special requirements, think about whether you need any more applications to support you.

Now, technical analysis for options trading is slightly different mainly because there is the subject of time decay in options. You cannot hold a position for an indefinite period of time. There is an expiration date for every option before which you will have to leave it. So, some of the common technical indicators that are used in this case have been discussed in the next section.

How to Get Started with Fundamental Analysis?

If you're anything like me, when you hear the word "fundamental analysis," you probably think about old men in suits with well-groomed beards and political ties. You may even make a reference to Gordon Gecko! But fundamental analysis isn't just for rich guys, it's an essential part of any successful trading strategy.

Here, I'll show you how to get started with fundamental analysis using some pretty simple steps:

1. Identify the market's trend.

It is important to determine whether the market is trending up or down before you begin your fundamental analysis. This is called trend identification.

Forex traders generally use several tools to determine the market's trend, such as:

- Simple moving averages (SMA) and exponential moving averages (EMA).
- Retracement levels and trend lines.
- Channels and triangles.
- Stochastic oscillators.
- High-low-close trading range indices.

When you attach a specific time frame to each of these charts, you'll have a more precise view of the market's trends; you can also figure out how much profit or loss your trading plan might create over an extended period of time with each of them.

2. Determine which technical indicators are most relevant to the market's trend.

For this, you'll need to practice more and more.

3. Calculate a risk.

You probably know the basic risk-reward principle (i.e., "buy low, sell high"). However, you should also be aware that the ratio between price and underlying value is not always close to 1:1.

For example, if a stock that's trading at $30 per share, you can expect it to return about 3 percent of your investment per year ($30 * 8% = $3 per year), but the stock could lose 10 percent of its value in one year ($30 * 10% = $3). In this case, you can gain much more than you lose from the investment if the risk is small.

The same idea applies to Forex pairs: If the price moves in a range of 0.1-0.2 pips, it's not a big deal; however, when price moves in a range of 1-3 pips, it will create a lot of noise in the spread (i.e., the difference between bid and ask). And when price moves into large ranges (5 pips or more), demand will be much higher than supply, resulting in a market imbalance that could result in slippage and potential losses.

4. Calculate a margin requirement for your position.

To calculate a possible loss, you need to figure out the maximum loss that your position will bring. You can do this by using logarithmic calculations.

For example, if you're trading a stock that's worth $100, and the market price moved up 0.2 pips today, then the stock is now worth

$102; in this case, your margin requirement will be $1 for every penny movement, no more no less.

5. Calculate an initial stop loss for each pair and set it on your chart.

"Stop" order is a command that tells your broker not to trade when a specific price has been reached.

You can use several types of stop-loss orders, but the most popular are:

•Stop-limit orders.

•Stop-loss orders.

•Stop-loss in points.

6. Calculate the exposure and risk capital before you enter a trade.

Some traders refer to this as an initial margin requirement or "margin." The professional forex brokers require your accounts to maintain a certain level of exposure in order to prevent any possible losses from running into your account's equity (e.g., the money you deposited into your account). Once again, it is very important that you make sure your margin requirement is greater than any possible loss that could run through the account and into negative territory.

7. Determine when you will sell your position.

This is easy, after you make some profit, of course!

8. Calculate the possible loss for each position you are in.

One of the best ways to analyze market risk is through a spreadsheet, which you can create with Microsoft Excel or Google Spreadsheets. Also, you can use an online forex calculator to calculate margin requirements and stop-losses without a spreadsheet: Forex Risk Calculator.

9. Decide whether or not your analysis makes sense for your trading plan, and adjust it accordingly.

Once again, I recommend that you start off with a simpler analysis, then proceed to a more complex analysis as your skills improve.

If you find it difficult to analyze a pair's strength and weakness, simply compare the present value of the Forex pair to price movement over a specified period of time. This is called "momentum."

Advantages & Disadvantages

For Fundamental Analysis:

Advantages:

- Only sound financial data are used to perform fundamental analysis. Thus, there is no scope of personal bias anywhere.
- You will arrive at a proper recommendation to either buy or sell by using analytical and statistical tools.
- Several long-term trends of demographic, economic, consumer, and technological origin are considered.
- Rigorous financial analysis and accounting pave the way for understanding everything in-depth and leaves room for no mistakes.
- Disadvantages:
- When you are considering the financials, some assumptions have to be made. So, I always advise everyone to consider both

the worst and best scenarios. There can be unexpected legislative or economic changes at any time.

- The entire process of industry analysis takes up a lot of time, and it is definitely not a cakewalk.

For Technical Analysis:

Advantages:

- You come to know the possible entry and exit points in the trade.
- You get to know how the overall market is performing, and you can judge the overall sentiments that are running.
- When you notice patterns, you can predict directions of movement.

Disadvantages:

- The underlying fundamentals are not taken into consideration while performing technical analysis. And thus, several risks can crop up because of this.
- Sometimes, if your chart is full of too many indicators, then the signals can be confusing.

INTRODUCING OPTIONS

What Are Options

Options are referred to as legal contracts that require the bearer to show enthusiasm towards a fixed price in acquiring or trading a large part of the asset. The individual holding the legal contract is authorized to buy the options or not, as long as the deal is yet to be completed. Options are sold as other asset groups, through portfolio brokers who are conversant with investment. Options are great to the extent that they could boost an individual's portfolio. By leveraging and including income protection, this can be achieved. Certain option circumstances can be in line with an investor's objectives, Depending on the current situation.

Let's assume that a share market is falling; options could be used as a possible hedge to reduce downside loss. One may use options to acquire continuous turnover. They can also be used for speculative motives, such as laying odds on the stock price. Just as free lunch in bonds and stocks doesn't exist, there are also no free lunches with options.

There are certain risks you may come across on the trading of options.

Before engaging in the trading of options, you must understand those risks. This explains why you are shown a disclaimer when you intend to trade options with a brokerage company that's familiar with all of this: options are partakers of a larger group of securities known as derivatives.

A derivative's price is linked with the cost of another item. To be more explicit, one type of tomato is ketchup. The equivalent of a grape is wine. A commodity derivative is a cash option. Options can be referred to as financial equity contracts, which means that their interest relies on the price of some currency. Examples of derivative products include calls, puts, advances, futures, and so on.

What is an Option Contract?

Option contracts are a way for investors to speculate on the price of underlying assets (stocks, commodities, etc.). The name given to the price of an option is called "strike." Options provide the holder with an agreement by the seller to buy or sell an underlying asset at a predetermined price.

A contract representing a stock option gives the holder the right, but not the obligation, to buy or sell an underlying stock at an agreed-upon price. The holder must own shares in the underlying security to exercise his or her option.

The market price of an option can be affected by many factors, and these factors, combined with the relationship of the strike price and stock price, will determine whether a call or put option is more valuable.

Options vs. Forex

An investor may presume that the U.S. dollar would get stronger as a comparison to the Euro, hence, the individual earns if what was earlier presumed turn out to be true. If the assumption turns out well, and the plan succeeds, it will continue to influence the trade. Once you become enthusiastic about trading options, you continue to get involved in acquiring and selling options on various numbers of futures, securities, etc., which can then rise or drop at a price over the process. It is similar to trading forex since you may easily manipulate the purchasing power to get a governing power over the economic future or stocks. There is a range of approaches in selling Options and making an investment in Forex. These approaches are as follows:

24/7 Trading

Investing in Forex rather than Futures, gives you the opportunity to make transactions as much as you can in a day, that is, all days of a week. The Forex sector is fast-growing and spreading like wildfire than any stock system you have come across on the globe. If you've decided to make a double-digit return on investment in the sector, it's imperative to have a fair time per week marked out to make certain trade transactions.

When an event occurs somewhere in the world, you may be fortunate to be among the first to profit from the foreign currency exchange incidence. You don't have to whirl away the time waiting to demand when the market will open up in the sector, unlike that of stocks for trading. You can conveniently deal with Forex if you decide to, at any hour of the day. You can even exchange it any time you so wish.

Fast Trade Completion

Taking advantage of the Forex trade market immediately allows you access to immediate trade actions. Unlike options and any other markets, you do not have to be postponed. When you put the request, it presents you with the most affordable and available quality on the market, rather than asking what company would end up buying. You won't be tempted to halt the process in the options scenario. As soon as you are a part of overseas trading platforms, contrary to the case of trading options, there's also a good chance for liquidity.

Non-Commission

Forex business doesn't require a fee because it is run like an interbank system, where investors are immediately linked with sellers. There are no instances in capital exchange and other sectors with trading commissions. You're going to see a gap between the asking price and the offer, that's how several Forex brokerages make their cool cash.

What Is a Broker and How to Select It

When engaging in day trading for a start, one of the most crucial decisions you are going to make is picking. This will determine the types of securities you can trade (for example, many brokers aren't going to work with cryptocurrencies for trading), how much you pay for each of your trades, and what kind of platform you use. Picking out a competent and experienced broker, who is easy to deal with can make a great deal of difference in the results you achieve with your trades.

When working with a broker, and having determined that they trade in the securities you are interested in, becomes their compensation plan. You want to know if it is going to be profitable for you and your trading pattern. Since day trading requires various minor transactions during the day, you don't want to have a compensation plan where the broker gets an already fixed payment every time you make a trade transaction.

There are varieties of different payment patterns that your broker can select, and you need to understand and accept the one you find most reasonable. Going with a fixed payment for the entire year would be nice, but you can also choose the payment pattern where your broker receives a particular commission from your earnings, so if you don't earn anything on a trade, you won't be running at a loss. Whichever broker you decide to go with though, make sure to let them know the payment pattern you would like to operate with them from the start.

One of the prerequisites you must consider when selecting a broker's company must include:

Margin and Account Necessities

The criteria for the accounts and the margin range among brokerages. Many investment companies may need initial minimum investments of $2,000, and others will need minimums of $10,000.

Margin criteria for stock options transactions depend on the trading company. The criteria for the investment margin can often differ as a result of the type of options approach that you want to use. For beginners, certain broker companies would ask you to sign a document showing your trading prowess in options.

Having completed the program and grasping extensively the methods that you plan to use, and have effectively traded paper, you will comfortably say that you are an expert in trading options. You can sell and acquire shorter and longer calls/puts while provided with margin rights. The contract that you sign is insurance for the trading company to be sure that margin-protected individuals grasp all the implications of the transactions they position. For example, in bullish economic conditions, an upcoming trader who sells naked calls might quickly hit a snag. If you were conversant with this course, you would be much less likely to position these trades because the potential risks are endless. Among the advantages of sharing trading, you will still be aware of the overall costs and potential earnings.

In case you are not buoyant enough to meet the requirements of your chosen brokerage company for maximum margin rights, you will still be able to purchase long calls and puts. Brokerage companies would usually require more money or better trading opportunities for short-selling calls and puts. If you find yourself in this situation, just divert the long calls and puts them into constructing your fund before you can organize a maximum margin-protected stock options account or find another brokerage company.

What Are Stocks

Stock is seldom called shares or equity. That is a sort of defense indicating an extent of control as it affects the company that issues it.

When an individual has stocks, he/she have the right to a portion of the company's earnings and assets. One can acquire shares and trade them at stock markets, but it doesn't imply that there are no other places to trade and acquire stocks. In private sales, too, stocks may be exchanged. In the business sector, there is hardly any investor that does not have shares in their portfolio. They will be in accordance with rules that regulate and protect consumers against depraved procedures until transactions can be treated as legal. Markets have exceeded them when compared with other financial products.

ADVANTAGES AND DRAWBACKS OF TRADING OPTIONS

Options trading is one way to invest in the stock market, and like anything, there are advantages and disadvantages to this investment route:

Advantages

Options trading is not a new thing, in fact, it has been possible for over thirty years, but it is only in the last ten years that it has become popular. This is because computers have made it easier for the average investor to access and understand this type of investment. It is complex and risky, but it can also be rewarding if used properly.

•Leverage

Trading in options allows the individual investor to position themselves in the stock market in the same way as someone with hundreds or thousands of dollars' worth of shares. However, if you are trading in options instead of actual share numbers, you have placed far less money at risk. You can effectively leverage a small number of funds to mimic a large share purchase.

•Risk

There is always a certain level of risk involved with investing in the stock market; no one can predict accurately what will happen to share prices in the future. However, options, if used properly, can help to reduce that risk. Purchasing options are much cheaper than purchasing shares, so you are not risking as much money per transaction. In addition, if you use the right strategy, as listed in the previous chapter; you can purchase several options which will act as a failsafe, limiting any potential losses.

It is possible to purchase shares and set a stop figure, at which point you will automatically sell the shares and minimize your losses. However, if anything happens which prevents you from accessing your account, especially overnight, the stock value can plummet, and your stop order will not have been able to protect you. If you had brought a put order for the value of your stop, then you will be able to minimize your losses simply by knowing what price you can sell your stock for.

•Returns Percentage

Because purchasing an option is much cheaper than purchasing the actual shares, as a result, you are unable to make the significant profits that you would make on a successful actual stock trade. However, the profits you do make offer a much better percentage return than the actual share price.

For example, if you purchase shares for $50 and the share price rises by $5 your percentage return is 10 percent. However, if you purchased an option for the sale number of shares, you may only spend $6 per option. When the price rises, you are set to make $5 per share, although this will be less when you take into account any cap placed on the option price increase. This may wipe a dollar off your return; you would only make $4 per share. As a percentage of the option purchase price, this equates to a 67 % return on your investment; significantly higher than if you had purchased the shares.

•Alternatives

One of the best and most important elements of trading in options instead of shares is the number of alternative options and trades which are available. The more you understand regarding options, the easier it will be to combine different puts and calls to create a profitable, yet protected scenario.

Options allow the knowledgeable investor to play the negative or downsides of a market; this is something that can often be tricky for individual investors trading through a standard brokerage. Options can also allow you to trade and make a profit from a stagnant market; one which is not moving in any direction. In many ways, trading in options will allow you to access the full range of possibilities which is simply not possible with standard stock investing.

•Software

Most stock market trading is completed via the internet as this gives you real-time access to the options available and up-to-date prices. To be able to access the prices and purchase, or sell, options and shares, you need to have a brokerage account. This means you will have access to their software and be able to use it to trade on the stock market. Alongside this, you will have a variety of spreadsheets and other calculators. All the software which you can use will provide you with an easy way to analyze the latest figures and movements before buying your options. The software will make it easier to pick your options and can even offer helpful hints and tips along the way!

•Direction

Trading in options allows you to potentially make money on the direction the market will travel in within any given timescale. Even if you are unsure whether to buy or sell, you will be able to purchase two or three options and cover your position whilst being ready to make a good return on your investment. Options allow you to trade whether prices are climbing, shooting down, or moving sideways.

This, like many of the strategies you can follow with options, will limit your exposure and potential losses. You can operate in the same way as though you were purchasing actual shares, but by trading, via options, you are reducing the risk of huge losses. It doesn't actually matter whether you are dealing with a bull market, bear market, or even a sideways market, options trading will allow you to trade, whatever the outlook.

•Passive Income

If you choose to use a covered call; or something similar on actual stock, it is possible to make a recurring, passive income without ever losing your stock. Of course, it is possible that someone will want to utilize their option to purchase your stock and you must be prepared to sell your stock. This is usually only an option if the stock rises dramatically in price, if you are expecting this kind of movement in the market and are not keen on losing your stock, there are other options to allow you to trade a rising market.

Disadvantages

Before you start trading in options, it is important to be aware of the disadvantages which this type of trading offers.

•Wasting Asset

An option has a limited life, all options come with an expiry date; after that, the option to purchase or sell shares expires, and you are left with nothing. The closer you get to the expiry date, the less the option will be worth, and it may be difficult to sell the option on, or even to make your money before the expiry date.

There is nothing you can do to adjust an expiry date so you must always watch your expiry dates and plan accordingly. In the worst-case scenario, a trade goes the opposite way to what you expect, and your options expire; leaving you with no way to recoup any of your outlay.

•Leverage

This has already been listed as an advantage, and it certainly can be.

However, it can also be a disadvantage as if you do not limit your exposure with your trading options the leverage you use to match a big share purchase can go against you and leave you facing a huge shortfall. This can be a much higher figure than you have available, and you may risk everything you own.

It is essential to be certain about what you are doing and the risk you're exposing yourself to before you enter any trade.

•Complexity

There is a huge range of variables and possibilities open to anyone trading in options. However, this means that there is a lot to learn before you can start trading in options. Unlike standard stock market trading, which can be learned in a few hours, it can take several months to fully understand the different options, how they work and in which combination you should use them.

This is a complex area of investing and done correctly, one which can provide a good rate of return on your investments. However, if done incorrectly, it can cost you the purchase price of your options or a lot more. It is essential to take the time to understand each trading scenario, when they are best used, and how you can mix and match them to get the desired result.

•Computers

A computer is a valuable asset and can assist with calculating possible outcomes as well as analyzing data. It is the best way to connect with the stock market as you can see exactly what is happening as it happens. However, if you are not familiar or are uncomfortable with computers, this can be a real downside as you will need to learn basic computer skills first. It is possible to learn to use a computer, but this will slow down your progress and ability to get started!

•Volume

There are some options available which are not used very often. Because of this, these options have little liquidity in them. This means that any spread offered will be cross a wide range, and it will be difficult, if not impossible, to make a reasonable return on this investment.

You should always check the volume of stock turnover before committing to a trade; it is best to avoid any stock which has a low turnover.

•Risks

Trading in options can be particularly risky for those who are new to investing. Even those who have been trading for years can be caught out. Options are supposed to be used to help to minimize any risk and balance a portfolio; however, if they are used incorrectly or without proper knowledge, they can be an exceptionally risky approach.

As with any investment opportunity, it is important to assess the potential risks before engaging in the activity. You should never commit funds that you are not prepared to lose. No matter how sure you are that you are right, there are many variables and factors which can change the landscape at a moment's notice.

•Ease of Access

Almost anyone can sign up for an online account and start trading. In fact, there are many emails and junk correspondence which advises people on how easy it is to open an account and be earning in no time.

Most of the software programs offer a free trial which allows you to watch the market and place dummy bets. The idea is to give you a feel of what it would be like and the tools which would be at your disposal. Of course, it is easy to play at investing, without thinking about it, you will gloss over any losses and focus on your wins. This is likely to convince you that you know what you are doing and start trading for real; where you may find it more difficult and harder to make any real money.

Starting trading in options has been made easy, especially by the high profile which has been adopted by binary options in recent years.

Unfortunately, this means that many people are creating online accounts and having a go, often resulting in them losing their money before they really understand the opportunities, they are investing in.

Investing should always be approached with your business head-on and a professional attitude; it is too easy to lose money by thinking you know what you are doing. Once you have understood the basics, it is important to start slowly and build your experience and knowledge; this will allow you to become a successful trader.

BASIC OPTIONS CHARACTERISTICS

What Is a Strike Price?

A strike price is a set price at which a subsidiary agreement can be purchased or sold when it is worked out. In the case of call options, the strike price is the position where the security can be bought by the option holder; in the case of fixed options, the strike value is the cost at which the security can be offered.

The strike price is also referred to as the exercise price.

Differences between the Strike Price and Stock Price

These two prices are usually the first thing that comes to mind when reviewing option trading. The strike price is what an option buyer pays, and the stock price is what they make based on how long the trade lasts (depending on their prediction). Understanding a few key points about these two prices can help you increase your odds for success.

The strike price is the value of an individual option contract. For example, a trader who purchases one AAPL at a $170 call contract will do so for $16/share ($1,020). If AAPL closes above $200 when expiration arrives, they'll have made roughly $830 per share ($2,070 profit) minus commissions. This is called the premium (discount) paid. The same option was purchased at $13/share ($0.65 per share). If AAPL closes above $200, they'll make $85 per share ($1,560 profit) minus commissions. This is called the intrinsic value (premium) earned.

On the other hand, the stock price is what a trader makes or loses based on how far out in the future their trade goes. With options expiring in real-time, you see exactly how your trade will perform when you buy it. You cannot predict stock prices, which is why options are referred to as time-dependent investments rather than security-dependent ones like stocks or bonds are. For example, a trader who buys one AAPL 170 call contract at $16/share earns a premium of $0.65 ($16/share - $13/share). If AAPL closes above $200 within the next month, they'll make $85 per share plus the premium of $0.65 ($85 + 0.65 = $87.50) minus commissions. This is called the intrinsic value (premium) earned and is the actual number that matters to option traders. This is also known as "real money" since you can actually cash these out on expiration day...and keep your profit.

Differences between the Strike Price and Premium Price

These two prices, though commonly confused, have very different meanings. Options traders will often call the premium price the strike price. The strike price is what a trader pays when they purchase an options contract, which they eventually hope to sell for a profit before the expiration day. The premium price is the amount of money that the trader makes or loses based on how long their trade lasts (depending on their prediction). Intrinsic value and time value are essentially synonymous with premium and money paid, respectively.

The last thing to note about premium prices is that they generally only exist in options that are in-the-money (ITM). For example, if you bought one AAPL 170 call option for $13/share ($0.65), and the stock closed above the strike price, then you'll make $13 per share ($0.65 per share - $16/share) minus commissions. In this case, your premium would be $0.65 per share (rather than $85/share). But if you sold that same option for $1,020 ($16/share), you'd only make $13 per share ($0.65 per share -$1,020). This is because the price of your AAPL 170 call option doesn't change until you sell it at expiration and collect on your profit.

Understanding Strike Prices

Strike prices are utilized in derivatives trading. Derivatives are financial items whose value is dependent on the underlying asset, generally another financial instrument. The strike price is the main factor of the cut and put option. For instance, the purchaser of an investment opportunity call would have the right, however not the commitment, to purchase that stock later on at the strike price. Correspondingly, the purchaser of an investment opportunity put would have the right, but not the commitment, to sell that stock later on at the strike price. The strike is the most noteworthy determinant of option value. Strike prices are developed when an understanding is first formed. It mentions to the financial specialist what price the underlying asset must reach before the option is ITM. Strike prices are normalized, which means they are at fixed dollar sums, for example, $32, $33, $31, $102.50, $105, etc.

The price distinction amid the strike price and the underlying stock price regulates an option's worth. When the strike price is above the underlying stock price, the option is OTM. For buyers of a call option. For this situation, the option does not have intrinsic value, however, it might even now have a value dependent on volatility and time until termination as both of these two variables could place the option in cash later on. Then again, If the underlying stock price is greater than the strike price, the option will have inherent value and be ITM.

A buyer of a put option will be ITM when the underlying stock price is lesser than the strike price and be OTM when the underlying stock price is greater than the strike price. Again, an Out-the-money option will not have intrinsic worth, in any case, it may, regardless, have value contingent upon the volatility of the underlying asset and the time left until the options end.

Expiration Date (Derivatives)

The expiry date for derivatives is the date set on which derivative contracts, such as options or futures, are substantial. Before this day, investors would have decided to manage their expiring role.

Before an option lapses, its proprietors can decide to practice the option, close the situation to understand their profit or loss, or let the agreement /contract expire worthlessly.

Basics of Expiration Dates

Expiration/Termination dates, and what they mean, differ reliant on the derivatives being exchanged. The termination date for recorded investment opportunities in the United States is ordinarily the third Friday of the understanding month or the month that the understanding lapses. On months that the Friday falls on a vacation, the lapse date is on the Thursday going before the third Friday. At the point when an option or futures contract passes its lapse date, the contract or agreement is invalid.

The most recent day to trade value options is the Friday preceding expiry. Along these lines, traders must choose how to manage their options by this last trading day.

A few options have a programmed exercise provision. These options are automatically practiced if they are in the money (OTM) at the hour of expiry. If a trader does not want the option to be practiced, they should finish off or roll the situation by the last trading day.

Index options likewise expire on the third Friday of the month, and this is also the last buying and selling day for American index options. In the case of European-type index options, the last dealing is usually the day before the expiration date.

Expiration and Option Value

All in all, the more extended a stock has to expiration, the additional time it needs to arrive at its strike price and, in this manner, the additional time value it has.

This is the reason the expiration date is so critical to options traders. The idea of time is at the core of what gives options for their worth. After the call or put expires, the time value doesn't exist. At the end of the day, when the derivatives lapse, the investor doesn't hold any rights that go along with possessing the call or put.

Significant: The expiration time of an options contract is the time and date when it is rendered invalid and void. It is more explicit than the termination date and ought not to be mistaken for the last time to trade that option.

CALL OPTIONS AND PUT OPTIONS

According to the rules governing options trading, whoever takes a purchase option on a house has not yet bought that house but has the option (the right) to buy the house within a specified period. In the financial markets, they pay an amount for an option to the person granting the right (the so-called option premium).

You cannot buy without a seller, so there are always two parties involved. The profit of one is losing another, and we call this a 'zero-sum game.'

However, both the buyer and the seller can earn money if the seller holds shares to cover the options. The profit on the shares then compensates for losing his option.

Call and Put

Call: A call has a right to an underlying buy at a convincing price within a specified period.

Sell: a sell is a right to an underlying asset to sell at a specific price within a certain period.

If you have a right, you can exercise it. If you have a duty, you are in a dependent position, and you have to wait for the counterparty to exercise its right. To acquire the privilege of the underlying, the buyer has to pay a premium to the seller (writer).

Remember, before entering a duty, you want a consideration, a payment, or a premium in money. Options are standardized products so that everyone can trade them at the same time on equal terms. For example, the same specifications apply to your neighbor with the same option as you (although the costs per broker can differ).

Options can be applied both defensively and offensively, depending on the objective of an investor. A defensive investor will use options differently than an offensive trader.

It is precisely that aspect that makes options a product that deserves a place in every investment portfolio. Options are the best invention after the wheel. Like with a wheel, you can also roll options to a later expiry date.

Realize that you can either buy or sell options during the entire term and don't have to wait until the last trading day.

Buy and Sell Call Options

The big difference between buying or selling options is that you buy a premium when you buy options. You receive a premium when you write, so there is a risk that the counterparty, so the buyer, can exercise his option if the expiration option has value.

Long Call (Buy A Call)

You can compare buying a call option with an option on a house: you may buy a house, for example, € 350,000 within a certain period. Suppose the house increases in value to € 400,000, you can exercise your purchase right, and you have a profit of € 50,000. In options trading, unlike a house, an option is not free, but the buyer must pay the price (the option premium) to the agent of the option.

Short Call (Sell A Call)

The seller has an obligation (but not the right) to deliver a fixed amount of an underlying asset at the agreed price, the exercise price. Sellers calling an option can best be compared with an insurer who speculates on the do not pass a certain event: an underlying rise above a certain price. Before you invest in options, it is essential that you first learn what the options are, but more importantly, what the risks are. There are investment services that work with options and claim that you need not know about options, but that you have to follow their advice. We think it is better that you know what you are doing. If the entrepreneurs had bought those interest rate derivatives on their bank's help, they would have done so because they would not have suffered substantial losses.

OPTIONS PRICE COMPONENTS. INTRINSIC VALUE AND EXTRINSIC VALUE

When you buy an option, you are paying a premium for the right to purchase or sell a stock at a specific time for a specific price. The price of an option consists of two components: intrinsic value and extrinsic value.

Intrinsic Value: is the difference between the market price of the underlying asset and the exercise (strike) price.

As a more theoretical explication, this is the value that a trader would have to pay to sell or buy shares at the strike price relative to their current market price. If you have a call option with a strike price of $50 on a stock trading at $80, your intrinsic value is $30. this means that the ability to buy the stock at $30 below the current market price, should be worth at least $30.

Extrinsic Value: The extrinsic value represents all other factors that contribute to the total cost of buying an option. It includes things like: interest rates, dividends, volatility, etc. Is the difference between an Option Premium Price and its Intrinsic Value.

OPTIONS MONEYNESS

An option contract's worth changes dependent on the cost of the advantage basic it, for example, a stock, trade exchanged reserve, or fates contract. The alternative can be in cash (ITM), out of the cash (OTM), or at the cash (ATM). Every last one of these circumstances influences the inherent estimation of the alternative.

The measure of time staying before the choice agreement lapses additionally assumes a job in the estimation of choice, which like these influences how high or low a value, the premium, the purchaser is eager to pay for the choice.

In the Money

If an alternative agreement is ITM, it has characteristic worth. A call choice, which gives the purchaser the privilege, however not the commitment to buy a benefit at a set cost before a specific day, is in the cash if the present cost of the fundamental resource is higher than that settled upon value, which is known as a strike cost. The purchaser could practice their privilege under the choice agreement and purchase the hidden resource for not as much as its present worth. That implies the call has inherent worth.

On the other hand, a put choice, which gives the purchaser the option to sell a benefit at a set cost at the latest a specific day, is ITM if the cost of the fundamental security is lower than the strike cost. The purchaser could practice their privilege under the alternative agreement and sell the basic resource for more than its present worth. That implies the put has inherent worth.

In outline, a call alternative is a wagered that the basic resource will ascend in cost at some point previously or on a specific day, known as the termination date, while a put choice is a bet that the basic resource's cost will fall during that time span.

If the strike cost of a call choice is $5 and the basic stock is at present exchanging at $6, the alternative is ITM. The higher above $5 the cost goes, the more ITM the choice is and the more noteworthy its characteristic worth.

On the off chance that the strike cost of a put alternative is $5 and the fundamental stock is at present exchanging at $4, the choice is ITM. The lower beneath $5 the cost goes, the more ITM the choice is, and the more prominent its inborn worth.

The natural estimation of an alternative that is ITM is the more prominent of the strike cost or the cost of the basic resource less than the other cost. Along these lines, the characteristic incentive for both the call and put alternatives with the strike cost of $5 is $1.

Out of the Money

On the off chance that a choice agreement is OTM, it doesn't have natural worth. A call choice is OTM if the present cost of the fundamental resource is lower than the strike cost. The purchaser of the call choice would not practice their privilege under the choice agreement to purchase the basic resource since they would be paying more than its present worth.

Then again, a put choice is OTM if the present cost of the fundamental security is higher than the strike cost. The purchaser of the put choice would not practice their privilege under the alternative agreement to sell the fundamental resource since they would not get as much as its present worth.

On the off chance that the strike cost of a call choice is $5 and the basic stock is at present exchanging at $4, the alternative is OTM. The lower underneath $5 the cost goes, the more OTM the choice is.

On the off chance that the strike cost of a put choice is $5 and the basic stock is at present exchanging at $6, the choice is OTM. The higher above $5, the more OTM the alternative is.

Since these OTM put and call choices cannot be practiced for a benefit, their natural worth is zero.

At the Money

If an alternative agreement's strike cost is equivalent to the cost of the fundamental resource, the choice is ATM. On the off chance that the strike cost of a call or put choice is $5 and the basic stock is presently exchanging at $5, the alternative is ATM. Since ATM put and call alternatives cannot be practiced for a benefit, their characteristic worth is additionally zero.

Time Value

The estimation of choice comprises both inborn worth and time esteem. The more prominent the measure of time until a choice terminates, the additional time esteem it has. That is because there is a more noteworthy possibility the choice will, sooner or later, become ITM over the more drawn-out time allotment before termination thus has natural worth.

When choosing the amount of a top-notch they're willing to pay, a forthcoming alternative purchaser must contemplate whether the fundamental resource has or is probably going to have natural worth and the choice's time esteem. An alternative can be OTM, and this way, have no natural esteem yet, at the same time, have to time an incentive up until its termination. If an ITM choice has $10 of inborn worth, the premium ought to be higher than $10 given the time esteem characteristic in the measure of time the basic resource needs to turn out to be much more ITM.

IMPLIED VOLATILITY

Volatility is an important input in the formula that is used for pricing options. It shows the magnitude of the variance that exists in the prices of an underlying security over a period of time. With that being said, how accurately can you predict the future based on the historical data? Let's take a closer look to understand some of the theoretical and practical concepts that help investment professionals enable the use of this powerful estimation tool.

Volatility Statistics

The most basic approach to calculating the volatility of a data set is by calculating the variance using its square root, the outcome is its standard deviation.

If we are looking to calculate the variance for a period of 15 days, we need to calculate the mean deviation of each day's specific stock prices. The second step is to square those deviations then divide the sum by the number of data items (in this case, 15). This will give us the variation. Although it is simple math, it can be confusing and tedious for newcomers. Thankfully using today's technology, spreadsheets help a great deal with such calculations.

The standard deviation that is derived from taking the square root of each point's variance from the mean is the volatility input. This input is used in the Black-Scholes option-pricing model.

When volatility is calculated by this standard deviation method, it is called historical volatility (i.e., using historical price returns and taking each return's variance from the mean, squaring that number, summing all of them, and then taking the square root of the sum). See below:

$$\sigma = \sqrt{\frac{\sum_{i=1}^{n}(r_i - \mu)^2}{n-1}}$$

Where:

Where:

σ = Standard deviation
r_i = Price returns
μ = Mean (average) of all data points
n = Number of data points

Note:

$$\mu = \sum_{i=1}^{n} r_i \quad \text{and} \quad r_i = \frac{(P_{i+1} - P_i)}{i}$$

Historical volatility example:

Let's look at S&P 500 price data for a 15-day period.

	Date	Close/Last	Mean Deviation	Deviation Squared
1	1/4/2019	252.39	2	6.2
2	1/3/2019	244.21	-6	32.3
3	1/2/2019	250.18	0	0.1
4	12/31/2018	249.92	0	0.0
5	12/28/2018	247.75	-2	4.6
6	12/27/2018	248.07	-2	3.3
7	12/26/2018	246.18	-4	13.8
8	12/24/2018	234.34	-16	242.0
9	12/21/2018	240.70	-9	84.6
10	12/20/2018	247.17	-3	7.4
11	12/19/2018	251.26	1	1.9
12	12/18/2018	255.08	5	26.9
13	12/17/2018	255.36	5	29.8
14	12/14/2018	260.47	11	111.8
15	12/13/2018	265.37	15	239.4
		Mean:	Average of Prices	250
		Variance:	Average of Dev. Sq.	53.6
		Standard Dev.	Sq. Root of Variance	7.32

Averages (interchangeable with "mean") in the example above can be calculated with a simple = Average formula. The mathematical foundation of this formula is summing each data point and dividing the total by the number of observations.

Similarly, you can use Standard Deviation and/or variance formulas to calculate the needed values directly in Excel.

Although it is a very useful concept, historical volatility can be misleading because markets frequently change in unpredictable ways.

Shortcomings of Historical Volatility

Historical volatility inherits an assumption that history will always repeat itself. Although this is true to a certain extent, there are always price movements and historical events that surprise even the most seasoned investment professionals. Historical volatility works well when predicting small price changes and trends over longer periods of time.

However, historical volatility is useless in predicting large directional changes in price. When something like this occurs, volatility immediately jumps significantly higher because of the change in deviation from the mean. If you are selling options against stock and the implied volatility (i.e., the volatility "implied" by the market) on those options spike, you will want to sell your options and collect the higher premium. If you have already sold your calls, a spike in implied volatility will make it considerably more expensive to buy the call options back. In this case, the best thing to do is nothing, remember that these options may become cheaper due to time decay, and regardless of that, our overall trading goal is to generate monthly income.

Other phenomena, even more unexpected, are black swan events. They were successfully theorized by economist Nassim Taleb, and they define events that are greatly beyond normal expectations of science, politics, technology, markets, etc. From this definition, we understand that if a topic is being widely discussed and predicted by many people, then it is not a black swan. Black swans catch everyone by surprise and are extremely unexpected in nature.

Emotional tip

Since historical data is not always a reliable metric to estimate the future volatility of an asset, what can be used to reinforce the future price predictions? Although it is an imperfect solution, implied volatility is a popular alternative to use in volatility calculations.

Implied Volatility

Implied volatility, a.k.a. the "market volatility" of an asset, is calculated by taking current option prices in the market and reverse-engineering the volatility input from those prices. Since an option's strike price, underlying price, interest rate, and time to expiration are certain values, it is relatively simple to use several iterations and extract an implied volatility value.

There are benefits and shortcomings of implied volatility. First, by checking the daily average movement of the market or stock, you are able to tell any volatility measures that are different than the theoretical historical volatility calculations. Thus, you can judge the potential future volatility of a stock or index by looking at the implied volatility of its options.

On the other hand, this can cause a "herd mentality" as everyone rushes to buy that option, therefore, driving the price higher than normal. If many people start judging the volatility only by implied volatility, this will create a closed-loop feedback system where everyone is relying on the same implied volatility values. For this reason, it is very important for options traders to remain critical as they calculate values for volatility; remember that these values are only an estimation of actual volatility. Another important and fundamental point to keep in mind is that volatility doesn't tell us the direction of price movements in a stock. Generally, in a flat market, a move in either direction would increase the volatility, thus causing a change in option values (all else constant).

Mini Glossary

Volatility:	A concept to measure the magnitude of price fluctuations.
Types of Volatility:	Historical, implied, stochastic
Other names:	Vol., IV (implied volatility), HV (historical volatility)
Symbol:	σ (Sigma)
Greek	Υ (Vega)
Volatility Indices:	S&P 500 Volatility Index (VIX) S&P 100 Volatility Index (VXO) Nasdaq 100 Volatility Index (VXN)

Knowledge Tip: What's the volatility change on a stock that is increasing 2% every day? (In a 90-day range)

The answer would be zero. Since a stock maintains the same level of change on a day-to-day basis, the variance and standard deviation would remain the same.

Volatility Indices

There are volatility indexes that are calculated by The CBOE Global Markets® (CBOE®). You can also find options and futures that use these index's as underlying securities.

US Volatility Indices

Delayed Quotes (7/5/2019)

Ticker	Index	Sym	Last	Pt. Change
VIX®	Cboe Volatility Index®	VIX	22.60	-2.54
VXN℠	Cboe NASDAQ Volatility Index	VXN	28.57	0.00
VXO℠	Cboe S&P 100 Volatility Index	VXO	24.38	0.00
VXD℠	Cboe DJIA Volatility Index	VXD	22.16	0.00
RVX℠	Cboe Russell 2000 Volatility Index	RVX	25.30	0.00

Volatility Indices on Non-U.S. Stock ETFs

Delayed Quotes

Ticker	Index	Sym	Last	Pt. Change
VXEFA	Cboe EFA ETF Volatility Index	VXEFA	18.07	0.00
VXEEM	Cboe Emerging Markets ETF Volatility Index	VXEEM	23.86	0.00
VXFXI	Cboe China ETF Volatility Index	VXFXI	25.03	0.00
VXEWZ	Cboe Brazil ETF Volatility Index	VXEWZ	34.57	0.00

Volatility Indices on Interest Rates:

Delayed Quotes

Ticker	Index	Sym	Last	Pt. Change
TYVIX	Cboe/CBOT 10-year U.S. Treasury Note Volatility Index	TYVIX	4.63	0.00
SRVIX	Cboe Interest Rate Swap Volatility Index	SRVIX	74.32	0.00

Volatility Indices on Commodity-related ETF's:

Delayed Quotes

Ticker	Index	Sym	Last	Pt. Change
OVX	Cboe Crude Oil ETF Volatility Index	OVX	51.52	0.00
GVZ	Cboe Gold ETF Volatility Index	GVZ	12.04	0.00
VXSLV	Cboe Silver ETF Volatility Index	VXSLV	21.70	0.00
VXGDX	Cboe Gold Miners ETF Volatility Index	VXGDX	31.76	0.00
VXXLE	Cboe Energy Sector ETF Volatility Index	VXXLE	29.95	0.00

Volatility Indices on Currency-related Futures/ETF's:

Delayed Quotes

Ticker	Index	Sym	Last	Pt. Change
EUVIX	Cboe/CME FX Euro Volatility Index℠	EUVIX	6.96	0.00
JYVIX	Cboe/CME FX Yen Volatility Index℠	JYVIX	9.48	0.00
BPVIX	Cboe/CME FX British Pound Volatility Index℠	BPVIX	13.03	0.00
Evz	Cboe Eurocurrency ETF Volatility Index	Evz	7.29	0.00

Volatility Indices on Single Stocks:

Delayed Quotes

Ticker	Index	Sym	Last	Pt. Change
VXAZN	Cboe Equity VIX® on Amazon	VXAZN	44.38	0.00
VXAPL	Cboe Equity VIX® on Apple	VXAPL	37.55	0.00
VXGS	Cboe Equity VIX® on Goldman Sachs	VXGS	36.60	0.00
VXGOG	Cboe Equity VIX® on Google	VXGOG	33.35	0.00
VXIBM	Cboe Equity VIX® on IBM	VXIBM	34.86	0.00

Volatility of VIX:		Delayed Quotes		
Ticker	Index	Sym	Last	Pt. Change
VVIX	Cboe VIX of VIX Index	VVIX	84.44	0.00

Source: The Chicago Board Options Exchange Website (CBOE.com)

Volatility – ETF Symbol = VXX – My Personal Favorite

This is the only option I buy in my personal account, and there is a very specific reason why…I have no idea when it's going to spike a market sell-off, however since I know the spike is caused by the implied volatility of the S&P 500 front-month put options, I know those put options will eventually revert back to the mean and the VXX will as well. To put it in simple terms, when the market starts to pull back, every novice trader goes out and buys put contracts on the S&P 500, the VXX tracks the pricing of those puts, and we just learned that implied volatility is simply the herd running from the lions which cause the price to go up. Give it a day or two and buy the following week ATM or ITM puts. As the market stabilizes and that protects those individuals, we mentioned earlier, begins to collapse, we would like to be on the put contract side. Never buy the calls unless you are hedging your portfolio when the market is at all-time highs. The people who bought the puts when the market pulled back or crashed bought at SUPER high prices.

Vega

Let's look at an option based on the NASDAQ 100 index, which tracks the top 100 stocks that are listed on the Nasdaq stock exchange. The PowerShares ETF QQQ ticker is an ETF based on the Nasdaq 100. While the Nasdaq 100 is just an abstract index calculation, QQQ can be bought and sold, thus trading the same way an individual stock trades.

There are options based on QQQ; let's analyze a few of them. As the underlying QQQ was trading around $156 that day, both options are at-the-money.

Option1: Mar 15, 2019 156.00 Call (#QQQ) is a call option with strike price of 156 and maturity date of 15th of March 2019.

Technical parameters

Delta0.79563
Gamma0.03777
Rho0.21842
Theta-0.10059
Vega0.18640

Option2: Mar 15, 2019 156.00 Put (#QQQ) is a put option with strike price of 156 and maturity date of 15th of March 2019.

Technical parameters

Delta-0.41405
Gamma0.02203
Rho-0.07932
Theta-0.04495
Vega0.24704

The call option has a Vega of 0.186, this means a 1% chance of volatility in the underlying price causes a $0.186 price change in the option. If volatility increased by 10%, the call price would increase by $1.86 in value (all else constant).

The put option, on the other hand, has a Vega of 0.247. Although volatility affects options pricing the same in both put and call options, Vega is higher here, therefore a 1% increase in the volatility would cause the option price to increase $0.247. The logic behind this difference is the thought that markets tend to sell off much more quickly and violently.

More Advanced Approaches

One big criticism of the Black-Scholes model is that it assumes volatility is constant throughout the life of the option. Although this was still a breakthrough in mathematics for option pricing, obviously, we understand that volatility is not a constant value. In fact, it changes at an instantaneous rate! Stochastic Volatility (SV) is one of the answers to this shortcoming of the other measures of volatility.

FOCUS ON EXERCISE AND ASSIGNMENT

Practicing options are used when you need to change over your options spot into stock. Most options brokers never really need to change over their options to stock; in this manner, practicing options are seldom used.

There are times you might need to claim stock by changing over your options. To practice your options, you must make a long put or a long call.

Short options never can practice their options; short options must be allotted.

To return to our options, a long put gives you the privilege to sell the stock, and a long call gives you the privilege to buy a stock.

You now are a long 1 contract of a TOP 40 call, and TOP is trading for $45. You concluded that you need to claim the TOP stock, so you practice the agreement. When you practice the agreement, you will buy 100 portions of TOP at $40 (the strike cost).

Presently, when you buy the stock, fight the temptation to go back and sell it for $45. If you plan to buy the stock and pivot and trade them for a benefit, you will prefer not to work out. You can accomplish similar outcomes with less expense if you offer to close your position.

When we look at practicing a long put, you will sell the offers as opposed to buying the offers.

You are long 1 contract of a TOP 30 put, and TOP is trading at $25. You choose to short the stock, so you practice your agreement. When you practice the contract, you will short 100 portions of TOP at $30 (the strike cost).

Much the same as with our long call, you would prefer not to practice the agreement so you can quickly close the position and gather the profit. If that were the situation, you would offer to close your long put. This will enable you to get the profit at a lower expense.

If you need to practice your option, you should contact the option company and let them know about your expectations. A few financiers will have catches to assign that you need to practice your option. However, most businesses will have you bring in to affirm your arrangements. Most financiers are going to charge you an additional expense to practice your options. You can rapidly observe and think about your financier expenses at StockBrokers.com.

If your options are one-penny in-the-money at lapse, it will consequently be practiced by your business. If you want to practice your options, you must finish it off with a buy to close or offer to close requests before termination. Holding up too long could be hindering your portfolio. You could rest on Friday with 5 entries that are marginally in-the-money and wake up Monday with 500 portions of stock in your portfolio.

Don't Exercise/Practice Out-of-the-Money Options

Never practice an out-of-the-money option. Practicing options are intended for in-the-money options as they were. This is effectively clarified with a model.

You now are long a call at 50 strikes. Your fundamental is at present trading at $40, and you choose to practice. Presently you have changed over your options into offers at $50.00 even though the basic is just trading at $40; you have a loss. If you needed to get the portions of the stock, you ought to have offered to close, finished off your options, and bought the offers in the market for $40 rather than $50. Try not to set yourself up by beginning with a loss, just options that are exercise in-the-money.

Don't Exercise an Option Before Expiration

When practicing your options before termination, you are giving up the properties of the options for which you've officially paid.

In the first place, you will relinquish the time price of the options. If your basic is trading at $50, and you're on a long call option at the $45 strike, you will have at any rate a $5 benefit (50 - 45). If you practice your options before the expiry, that is your lone benefit on that position.

If you have time to stay before the lapse, your call will have a greater benefit without anyone else's input. The benefit of your call would be $5 + time value. When you practice, you lose the time value.

You could offer to close the options in the market for more than $5 if it is before lapse. The closer you get to lapse, the more your time worth abatements until it comes to $0. Your call would be worth $5 at termination, and that is the point at which you practice.

You are long an approach the $30 strike that costs $3.00 and terminates in about 14 days, and your fundamental is trading for $40. You concluded you're close enough to lapse and need to practice your call. You never again have those options and now hold 100 offers at $30. The following day an unexpected declaration is discharged that the organization is under scrutiny for misrepresentation. The stock starts to sink, and toward the day's end, it worth $20. You are presently sitting on a $1,000 loss. If you had held those options, it would be useless now. However, your all-out loss would have just been $300.

Even though you will begin your options instruction by finding out about practicing options at the strike value, you will find that you will occasionally practice genuine positions. Most options brokers never need to claim the stock. They trade options to deal with the agreements forward and backward.

When you buy to open, go long, or pay a net charge for a position, go long or open; you will use an offer to near close the position.

If you offer to open, go short, or get a net acknowledgment for a position, you will use a buy to near close the position.

Options aren't as risky as Wall Street would make it look. Infect, they can limit risk. Here is an options trading strategy that can enable you to get huge twofold digit gains and overcome any potential losses.

Two rules or guidelines to follow every time you want to make a trade are:

- Practice before spending real money on live trades.
- For any trade, risk no more than 2% of your wallet.

Occasionally, however, you may detect a deal that you have faith in your heart can profit from.

The main issue is it costs more than $500.

So, would you be able to, in any case, make a profit without totally overlooking risk management? The appropriate response is yes! Here's the ticket: Use put or call debit spread to hedge risk on a highly-priced option

Remember that your profit potential is boundless when buying calls, however your most extreme benefit potential when buying puts is constrained since the stock can just drop as low as zero. The most you stand to risk (or loss) on a long call is the measure of money you spent to gain entry to the trade. As said before, you only get to lose the money you spent on the trade, which is the only risk involved.

In a debit put or debit call spread, what you're doing is "selling to-open," an option opposite the one "bought to-open," which supports the danger of your trade. This implies you're at the same time selling and buying either puts or calls (on a similar request ticket) to counter-balance the expense of puts or calls bought.

Asides from those, diagonal spreads are a magnificent long-haul approach to both contribute with options and produce some month-to-month income simultaneously. Numerous merchants don't think a lot about how ground-breaking and adaptable these spreads can be for fruitful trading.

Diagonal option spreads are built up by getting into both a short and long position in two options of an identical sort (either two put or two call options) yet with various strike costs and termination dates.

Take one moment to process that and read it again if you must. The technique is like a covered call, then again, a long call is replaced with the stock.

This technique is called "diagonal" since it joins a level spread, which speaks to contrasts in lapse dates, with a vertical spread, which speaks to contrasts in strike costs. You could even consider it the posterity of vertical and calendar spread.

How and When to Use a Diagonal Spread

One of the essential reasons you might close a diagonal spread is if you want to procure enough premium from the subsequent barter. Then again, you might be provoked to closing the trade should the close month option seem to go in-the-money, and you need to keep away from the capability of getting relegated on the sold options.

The following are a couple of investments to pursue when hoping to close a diagonal spread.

Get into a buy-to-close request for the close termination contract that you had recently sold.

As a standard guideline, it is significant for you to, in every case in a diagonal spread, close the short side first for edge prerequisite reasons.

Assess the benefit capability of the long option that is staying in the exchange.

Now, what you must decide is whether the fundamental security is probably going to move the correct way. If you possess a call contract, then you will trust that it climbs. Then again, you will foresee that it goes down if you possess a put option.

BUYING OPTIONS VS. SELLING OPTIONS

If you invest in stocks, you often have some sort of "buying" or "selling" option.

What are Buying Options?

Buying Options are basically the right, but not the obligation, to buy stocks in a company at a set price.

What are Selling Options?

Selling Options are options that allow you the right, but not the obligation, to sell any stocks you have in a company at a set price. They are often available for an extra fee.

Buying Options VS. Selling Options

You can buy or sell options on any stock.

For example, JKLM is J.C. Penney Company, Inc. (NYSE: JCP).

You can buy the stock at a cost of $50/share for a Total Premium of $50 (Cost + Option Premium), and you get the right to buy it at $52/share for a Total Premium of $2 (Payout + Commission).

The above would give you an investment that would grow to $53 if you stayed with the stock while growing at 12% annually for 20 years.

So, you save $1 when you buy the option as opposed to buying the stock at full price.

If you sell the stock prior to expiration for a profit, you will have to pay a commission of $10/trade and a percent of the amount.

So, in this example, if you bought the stock at $52 and sold the option for $55, you would still be charged a $10/trade commission and a 6% fee or $1.50.

This would leave you with an investment worth about: $53 - ($2 +$1.50) = $48.50 and growing at 12% annually for 20 years would leave it worth about: $48.5 - 1.50 = $46.50

This is a net loss of $1 on the investment and an effective yearly loss of $2.

What is the difference between Buying Options and Selling Options?

It really comes down to a company's dividend policy and stock price.

If the company has a "no dividends" policy, selling options will have a higher premium than buying options.

Examples:

To properly use options to maximize returns, one must keep in mind that options are not risk-free investments, in that one is exposed to significant market risks when purchasing an option contract. One must also understand the potential consequences of owning an option contract. For example, if the owner of an in-the-money call option suddenly needs cash and liquidates the position, then there will be a transaction fee along with a loss equal to all of the premium paid to purchase the option.

Also, predictions about future stock prices can be very difficult. It is not uncommon for investors to see stock prices suddenly fall after they buy options because they did not take into account certain factors that caused them. For example, an investor may have bought a call option on Company XYZ because he thought there was going to be a positive earnings announcement from XYZ within several weeks. However, the announcement actually came two weeks later than expected, and the stock price of XYZ fell, which decreased the value of the call option. In this situation, an investor will suffer a loss on their purchase of the option. The option owner can recover some or all of his losses by selling their position before it expires.

Although many options are traded in a cash-settled manner, there are also over-the-counter options that are not based on an exchange clearing system. These over-the-counter (OTC) options are subject to greater market volatility than standardized options. This is due to differences in underlying markets and other factors such as derivative types such as credit default swaps (CDS).

One options strategy that has recently gained popularity is the binary options trading strategy. Binary options are a derivative over traditional stocks and index options. The general idea of binary options is that the investor places a highly specific bet on the direction of a certain asset (such as a share price, index, or market event such as an election). The bet needs to be correct within a set time limit. If the investor achieves their desired result, then they profit accordingly, usually at set increments up to 80% or more return on investment.

THE OPTIONS GREEKS

When you begin options trading, you are going to encounter some mysterious parameters called "the Greeks." These are five pieces of data that accompany every option, and they are denoted with Greek letters. The designations used are a result of the mathematical formulas that go into options pricing, but don't let that put you off. Many options traders don't pay much attention to the Greeks, but as a more informed options investor, you are going to want to, at least, be aware of them and check their values.

The first thing to know about the Greeks before we get started looking at them in detail is that they change in real-time. So, if someone tells you that delta is 0.5 or 0.62, it doesn't mean these are going to be the values that you see by the time you look at the option. As the stock trades all day long, and the value of the share price changes, the values of the Greeks are going to change as well.

Delta

The first Greek that we are going to encounter is named for the Greek letter delta. This parameter tells you how the price of an option is going to change with respect to a change in the share price of the underlying stock. It is listed as a decimal number that ranges from 0.0–1.0.

The dividing line for delta is 0.50, which is the value delta would have for an option that was exactly at the money. So, what does this mean? It means that if the price, for instance, goes up by an increment of $1.00, you are looking at a call option that is $0.50 more. So, if the share price of Disney happened to be $132, and you possess a call option having the exact price, if the share price went up to $132.50, the price of the call option would go up by $0.25. On the other hand, if the share price had risen to $133, the value of the call option would have risen by $0.50.

While traders like to focus on gains, this cut both ways. So, if the stock dropped from $132 a share to $131 a share, your option would drop in value by $0.50.

Remember that options prices are quoted on a per-share basis, but they are for 100 shares of stock. That means that a 50-cent drop is quite significant. If you're looking at an option that is priced at $100, a 50 cents drop in share price could translate into a drop in the price of the option of $25. And of course, if it rose by $0.50, you'd make $25 on the option.

Put options have a negative delta. This reflects the fact that the correlation between the put's value and the fluctuation in the share's price is in the opposite manner. That is, if the price of the stock goes up, the put option loses value. If it's another way around; that is, the stock loses its favorable spot in the market, the put options become lucrative when traded. But the meaning is the same.

So, when you are looking for an at-the-money put option, you are going to see a delta of -0.50. If the price of the stock rises by $1, you will lose 50 cents per share on the option. In contrast, if the stock dropped by $1 in value, you would gain fifty cents.

Remember, with put options, there is a negative sign. So, an in the money put option will have a value that is more negative than -0.50. If you see a put option with a delta of -0.65, which means it's in the money. If you see a put option with a value of -0.25, that indicates that it is out of the money. In any case, for a put option, the key to remember is that if stock prices rise, put option prices drop. When stock prices decline, put option prices rise.

Theta

The second Greek that you want to keep an eye on is theta. This is a measure of time decay for the option. Theta is always negative. This reflects the fact that as time goes on, the value of the option that is tied up in time value declines. The time value of an option always declines; the question is only by what amount. You can look up theta to determine the amount. As stocks are traded throughout the day, the value of theta is going to change. However, the way that you are going to feel theta is when the days' pass. So, at each market open on a new trading day, options will lose extrinsic value. The amount of value that they lose will be equal to the value of theta.

If you look up an option that is priced at $1 (per share), and you see theta is -0.11, at market open, the value of the option will drop to $0.89. In real terms, if you had bought the option for $100, it would drop in value to $89.

However, you definitely need to account for that loss, so theta is not something to ignore. If the option is out of the money, it's going to be harder to make up for the value lost in the option due to time decay.

That illustrates how theta works. It's going to make its impact felt at the market open. Options do not lose time value during the day; it's the number of days to expiration that is important. The fewer the number of days left to expiration, the less time value the option has. As it loses value each day, we say that the option is experiencing time decay. All options go through time decay, no matter what. Since it's the number of trading days left to expiration that determines this, it only applies as the market opens.

Vega

The third most important Greek (in my opinion) is Vega. This Greek parameter tells you how sensitive the option is to changes in implied volatility. Precisely, the value of Vega estimates how the price of the option is going to change in response to a 1% change in the implied volatility of the underlying stock. Under normal conditions, Vega may not be that important. While you can look up the volatility for a given stock by looking at its beta parameter (note that beta is for the stock itself, not for options), that gives you the long-term volatility of the stock. Over short time periods, under most conditions, the volatility is not going to change all that much.

However, there are certain conditions under which the volatility can go up significantly, and this can have a large impact on share prices and on the value of options. One situation that you can look for this to happen is when there are approaching earnings calls for a heavily traded stock. When there is an upcoming earnings call, implied volatility, which means the future volatility, is going to go up by a large margin. So, while implied volatility can be taken to be relatively constant during normal trading times, in the week or two leading up to some earnings call, it can go much higher, and this can cause a dramatic spike in options prices. Remember that the price of the option is simply influenced by higher levels of volatility. More implied volatility means higher options prices, period. That's because it means there is a higher probability that an option could move in the money.

Rho

Is a Greek parameter related to the risk-free interest rate? The risk-free interest rate is usually taken to be the interest rate on a 10-year U.S. Treasury bill. What is important for options is not the interest rate itself but how it is changing. Rising interest rates can make options less attractive because capital tends to leave the stock market and go into bonds when interest rates are rising by large amounts. In today's environment, and, in fact, over the past 20 years, this hasn't been too much of a concern. Interest rates have been at record low levels over the past decade, as government officials have been trying to use low-interest rates to prop up the economy. Whether that actually works or not is not our concern here, but the fact of the matter is they have only tentatively raised interest rates at times that they have considered doing so, which means that the impact on the stock market has been minimal.

If there is a market crash, this is another situation where many traders and investors will move their money out of the market and possibly into 'safe' investments like bonds. That could be another situation where you want to keep an eye on rho, and also keep an eye on what the Federal Reserve is going to be doing with interest rates. This can actually represent an opportunity to get into options trading because they may actually lower interest rates in order to stimulate economic activity, making options more attractive.

If inflation is rising, this can also cause problems for options traders. The Federal Reserve tries to target a 2% inflation rate. If inflation rises dramatically or goes higher than this, that can mean they will push up interest rates to make money more expensive. In turn, this will mean rho is going to rise, and options are going to be less attractive because, once again, higher interest rates mean capital moving out of the stock market and into bonds. This type of movement hadn't happened very significantly since the late 1970s and early 1980s when inflation was very high, and interest rates were lifted dramatically to bring it under control. But if you are going to become a full-time options trader, you need to be aware of how it works in case you run into this type of situation during your trading life.

Gamma

The final Greek is called gamma. Simply put, or maybe not simply put, if you are not mathematically minded, gamma is the rate of change of delta. Technically, it's the second derivative. It tells you how rapidly delta is going to change with changes in stock prices. While hardcore options traders are going to be paying attention to this, most options traders don't need to keep a close eye on gamma. Beginning options traders are probably only going to be looking at delta and theta, and my experience is that delta provides the real information that you need when it comes to the sensitivity of the option to changing stock prices. Rather than the following gamma, you are better off keeping tabs on the delta in real-time. The odds are that delta is not going to change much unless there is a very large change in stock prices.

OPTIONS TRADING. THE ESSENTIAL GUIDELINE

You already know some of the basics that come with working on options as well as some of their benefits. Now it is time to learn how to get started with options so that you can make the money that you want.

But that does not mean that there are no risks involved. Almost every investment entails a multitude of risks. The same goes for options. An investor ought to know of these risks before proceeding with trade.

Getting It All Started

You may be excited to jump into the market and start trading right away, but there are a few things that you will need to do first. You will need to start out with a good understanding of the basics that come with options, and you need to know some of the option types that you can pick from. We talked about these topics a little bit before, but the more that you can learn about them before investing, the more success you will have.

After you have had some time to understand what options all are about and what you will be getting yourself into, it is time to come up with your motivation for trading. Ask yourself how much money you are looking to make from this trade and how you would like to use that money when you have earned it. This motivation is going to help you out so much when you are in the thick of the trading, and you need some help staying focus.

But one of the most important things that you will need to focus on when you first get started is having what is called a trading plan. The trading plan is going to basically list all the things that you want to be able to accomplish while you are trading. It can include what you expect to happen, some of your goals, the strategy that you will go with, and any other guidelines that will help you be successful. Those who decide to start investing in options without having a good plan in place will be the ones who run into a lot of risks.

Determine Whether You Will Proceed as a Company or an Individual

Both these alternatives are a lot different when actual options trading comes into practice. The legal obligations of both vary significantly. Besides, check whether you can trade with an offshore company or an offshore bank account. This could be advantageous in some tax-related situations. Non-resident citizen offshore companies and bank accounts are quite beneficial.

Get A Trading Account

Setting up an online trading account is the foremost thing to do when starting trading in options. Step-by-step instructions are provided by companies, which makes it extremely easy to manage the account. But this process does take some time, so start early.

A lot of factors are taken into consideration while deciding on your trading account.

The amount of money you are planning to invest in is the first thing that defines the type of account, which will be opened.

A very modest amount of start-up money is required to start trading in stock only. Even 200$ will work. But a Basic options account requires a minimum start-up of 2000$. If you have enough capital, setting up a day-trading account shall be an optimal choice. This account enables you to buy and sell as many times as you want.

Another choice one may get is if they want to open a margin account or not. A Margin account has its benefits.

After selling a stock or option, you get the money immediately, which in turn enables you to buy again. Some time is required in a regular account to clear the proceeds from a sale. A Margin Account enables you to borrow money to trade while using your own capital at the same time. One can say that it is, like an overdraft facility, which allows you to get extra funds.

There is a catch, though. A margin account requires a lot of time to be approved. You can start with a regular account and apply for a margin account later. You must use your own money in a regular account, and setting it up is less time-consuming.

The Need for Research Companies and Their Relevance

Acquiring the best research information can be a tedious task. The market has a lot of research groups. To make successful trades and make your ventures profitable, up-to-date information about options is of utmost importance. One needs to be completely aware of the existing market conditions. So, you can look for companies that provide this information and make more informed decisions.

Select a Security

This can be done by researching the finance sections of major news corporations. A simple search will turn up results such as CNN's Money section, which lists the most active companies according to the S&P 500. If the investor is already partially immersed in the finance world, it would be wise to seek out the advice of a friend or mentor. New options traders, and particularly those who are new to trading in general, should approach options trading cautiously. Rather than diving right in, investors should get their feet wet by experimenting with a limited number of securities and options so that they can keep track of gains and losses and avoid mistakes for future investments.

Choose OTC or Regulated Trading

But first, what are OTC and Regulated Trading?

A trader who buys and sells securities for their own account.

The job of the market maker is to provide continuous two-way quotes, depth of market, and liquidity within a pre-defined range. They do this by taking the opposite side of customer orders or by buying at the bid price when there are no other sell orders to take an order from. Market Makers want to keep the volume in their quotes because volume creates liquidity that traders want in order for trading to be more efficient. In the exchange, they charge a small fee called "markup." This quote is usually converted into points so that it easy for customers to understand what they are paying per point (e.g., 10,000 points = $100,000 value).

What is an OTC or over-the-counter trade?

A trade between two parties who are not members of a stock exchange. OTC trades can only be done at a set price. It can be exactly the same as trades on the NYSE (a matter of 0.01 cents). The difference is that OTC trades are not reported to the SEC like stocks and bonds. They are only reported to individual investors. OTC trades can be done within a specific range of price, or over a much bigger range of price. The OTC trading system is usually a little easier to use than the stock exchange because you don't have to be a member of an exchange to trade on the exchange.

Goldman Sachs once wrote that "the greatest attraction of OTC trading for market makers is that they make their money in another way." Since market making can be a very profitable business, many market makers prefer it because they can make payments with their profits which they hope will always exceed their annual expenses.

The difference between OTC and regulated trading is that the SEC regulates OTC trades. Both types of trading are risky, but regulated trades are much riskier than OTC trades because they are reported to the SEC and can be regulated with money.

While this can be decided at a later stage, it is suggested here, so that new investors can refer to the boards of a regulated exchange, such as the New York Stock Exchange, when choosing a put or call that is well suited to their tastes. Practiced traders can pick up an OTC option later if desired, such as a call to cover the cost of an insurance put, also known as a married put.

Select Strategies

Before beginning trading, investors will need to be sure they are familiar with a few simple strategies that can be implemented with a stock.

Examine the Market

Investors will need to study the time frame charts associated with their underlying security selection. Consider all three trends regarding the time frame and note how the security is moving within each.

Purchase Options and Trade

Finally, the moment investors have been waiting for. Based upon conclusions drawn from studying time frame charts, investors will need to buy the appropriate calls or puts. At the same time, investors should choose one or two of the strategies with which they are already familiar that they believe will work well in the present market climate. If trading via a regulated exchange, options for the strategies may be selected from a list published by the exchange.

Getting a Broker

Interactive Brokers are favorable in case you open only one account. They offer quick options information while being less expensive than other alternatives.

A lot of online brokers can be found, but they charge a certain amount for their services, which can affect your profit margin in the initial stages of trading.

The broker is going to be the person who works with you and often will be able to give you advice and help you to make the trades that you want. All brokers that you go with will require some fees or a commission that you will need to pay to use their services, so you must factor this in when figuring out the costs that you want to incur. There are many different types of brokers that you can go with and the price that you pay will depend on the type and number of services you choose to go with.

When you pick out the broker you want to work with, you will probably need to meet with them in the beginning and discuss your trading plan and how they will be able to help. They will go over a risk assessment with you, so they know where you stand with the number of risks that you are willing to take. It is a good place for you and the broker to get started together so you are on the same page and can get things done.

Appreciate That Options Trading Is Not Simple

It is vital at this stage to recapitulate the meaning of options trading. This is a contract that grants one the right to either buying or selling security based on the speculative value of it in a limited period. However, the contract is not obligatory in nature. In understanding options trading, two forms of it must be understood; first is a call option, and the other is the put option. The two are opposites of each other. One buys the former option when one expects an asset's value to go up over time but before the deadline of expiry of the contract expires.

However, participating in this market requires one to have enough understanding of how it works. Any venture requires one to learn enough. Educating oneself generally about investment is the best standing point. This creates understanding and ensures that one can comprehend the way that the options trading market as an investment venture works.

Among the reasons why people should educate themselves on options trading is because it does not work in certain ways. It also does not have guarantees of profit. This means that it, just like other ventures, involves risks that should be understood. The risks in the case of trading options are quite extreme. It requires calculation and being accurate as one speculates about the drop and rising of the value of the options on offer. Being interest in a venture that involves a high-risk level requires enough knowledge and sometimes mentorship by those who have prior knowledge and understanding of the market to avoid plunging into frustration and wastage of capital.

OPTIONS TRADING TIPS AND TRICKS

Inexperienced traders are often warned away from purchasing options that are out of the money as being a greater risk than the ultimate reward is likely to be. While it is true that a short expiration time coupled with an out of the money option will frequently look appealing, especially to those with a smaller amount of trading capital to work with, the issue is that all of these types of options are likely to look equally appealing, which leaves them with no way to tell the good from the bad.

As a more experienced trader, however, you have many more tools at your disposal than the average novice, which means that, while risky, cheap options have the potential to generate substantial returns, as long as you keep the following in mind while trading them.

Ignoring the Statistics Behind Options Trading

One of the biggest mistakes that most newbie options traders make is that they forget the probability is a real thing. When you check a potential stock before purchasing an option, it's important to understand that the history of an option is important when deciding whether or not you should be investing in it, but so are the odds and probability surrounding whether or not a particular event is going to occur.

For example, a common strategy that investors use is to leverage their money by investing in cheap options so that this will help to prevent big losses on a stock that they actually own shares of. Of course, this is a good strategy, but nothing works 100 percent of the time. Make sure that if the rules of probability and simple ratios are telling you to stay away from a deal, you listen to the facts staring you in the face. Wishful thinking will come to bite you later on.

Being overzealous: Oftentimes, when new options traders finally get their initial plan just right, they become overzealous and start committing to larger trades than they can realistically afford to recover from if things go poorly. It is important to take it slow when it comes to building your rate of return, and never bet more than you can afford to lose.

Regardless of how promising a specific trade might seem, there is no risk/reward level at which it is worth considering a loss that will take you out of the game completely for an extended period of time. Trade reasonably and trade regularly, and you will see greater results in the long-term guaranteed.

Not Being Adaptable

The successful options trades know when to follow their plans, but they also know that no plan will be the right choice, even if early indicators say otherwise. There is a difference between making a point of sticking to a plan and following it blindly and knowing which is one of the more important indicators of the separation between options trading success and abject failure. This means it is important to be aware of when and where experimentation and new ideas are appropriate and when it is best to toe the line and gather more data in order to make a well-reasoned decision.

This also means having several different plans in your options trading toolbox and not just resolutely sticking to the first one that brings you a modicum of success. This is crucial as there are certain plans that will only work in specific situations, and knowing which to use when, in real-time, will lead to significantly greater returns on a more reliable basis every single time.

Likewise, an adaptive options trader knows that market conditions can change unexpectedly and is prepared to respond accordingly. This means understanding when the time is right to go in a new direction, regardless of the potential risks that doing so might entail.

Sometimes a good trader has to make a leap of faith, and a trader who is successful in the long term knows what signs to look for that indicate this type of scenario is occurring in real-time. Unfortunately, this type of foresight cannot be taught, and instead must be found with experience.

As long as you keep the appropriate mindset regarding individual trades, any new strategy that is attempted will result in valuable data, if nothing else. It is important to understand that learning not to use a specific course of action a second time is always valuable, no matter the costs. Working to build this into your core trading mindset will lead you to greater success in a wider variety of situations in the long term.

Ignoring the Probability

Always remember that the historical data will not apply to the current trends in the market at all times, which means you will always want to consider the probability as well as the odds that the market is going to behave the way it typically does. The odds are how likely the market is to behave as expected, and the probability is the ratio of the likelihood of a given outcome. Understanding the probability of certain outcomes can make it easy to purchase the proper options to minimize losses related to holdings of specific underlying stocks.

When purchasing cheap options, it is important to remember that they are always going to be cheap for a reason as the price is determined by the strike price of the underlying stock as well as the amount of time remaining for the option to regain its value, choose wisely otherwise you are doing little more than gambling, and there are certainly better ways to gamble than via options trading.

Not Considering Exotic Options

An exotic option is one that has a basic structure that differs from either European or American options when it comes to the how and when of how the payout will be provided or how the option relates to the underlying asset in question.

Additionally, the number of potential underlying assets is going to be much more varied and can include things like, what the weather is like or how much rainfall a given area has experienced. Due to the customization options and the complexity of exotic options, they are only traded over-the-counter.

While they are undoubtedly more complex to get involved with, exotic options also offer up several additional advantages when compared to common options, including:

- They are a better choice for those with very specific needs when it comes to risk management.
- They offer up a variety of unique risk dimensions when it comes to both management and trading.
- They offer a far larger range of potential investments that can more easily meet a diverse number of portfolio needs.
- They are often cheaper than traditional options.

They also have additional drawbacks, the biggest of which is that they cannot often be priced correctly using standard pricing formulas. This may work as a profit instead of a drawback, however, depending on if the mispricing falls in favor of the trader or the writer.

It is also important to keep in mind that the amount of risk that is taken on with exotic options is always going to be greater than with other options due to the limited liquidity each type of exotic option is going to have available.

While some types are going to have markets that are fairly active, others are only going to have limited interest. Some are even what are known as dual-party transactions, which means they have no underlying liquidity and are only traded when two amiable traders can be found.

OPTIONS TRADING STRATEGIES

It specifies what you wish to do with your options and how long you want to trade in them. You must also know how much you are looking at making so that you can dispose of your options as soon as you reach your end goal. A strategic plan will be a tool that you can use to know about the resources that are at your disposal and how well you plan on using them. They will help you achieve whatever you wish to from the markets while cutting down on loss potential.

Trading strategies can help people get what they want from their trades and why they are trading in the first place. It helps in outlining the various steps that are involved in evaluating, executing, and taking care of your options portfolio. Before you get started with it, there happen to be a few things that you need to know or develop before initiating the trade.

One thing to understand is that just because you have a good strategy in place does not mean that it will always work out in your favor. You might run into some issues and end up losing a little on your profit. You have to be prepared for it and have a few plans in place that will help you offset it.

It might be quite simple to develop a strategy that is unique to you. All you have to do is spend some time thinking about the strategy that will work for an investor of your caliber. Remember that no one strategy will work for all, and it is all about finding your path. To help you come up with some of these strategies, these will highlight some tips for you. Before that, let us look at the benefits of strategic planning.

•There is a vast difference between making plans in advance and acting impulsively. If you have plans in place, then you will be able to take the right steps when there is a need to do so. In short, strategic planning can help you invest the money that is at your disposal and make the most of it. You, therefore, have to be proactive and not reactive.

•You must have a plan of action and ensure that you attain the goals that you set out to achieve. If you keep waiting for things to fall into place, then it will not work out and take forever for it to happen. But if you take action now, then you will be able to capitalize on the opportunity and ensure that you set up an ideal market for yourself. You do not have to be scared of the market, pulling up a sneaky one, and be prepared for all the things that might come your way.

•A strategic plan will guide you and prepare you for any emergencies. As you know, it is impossible to understand how markets can operate, and it is vital to be ready for whatever comes your way. If you make the effort of putting a plan in place, then it will work in your favor. You can have a sense of direction and know exactly which way the markets will move and whether you are prepared for it.

•The key is to understand that there will be many scenarios in the market, and it will be impossible to know which way things will move. You have to have a clear understanding of what you wish to achieve and why you want it. These might sound too basic, but it is essential to answer these questions if you're going to make the most of your options trading strategies. You should know exactly how much you will be investing and where. It will give you a good idea of the resources that are at your disposal and how best they can be employed. It will prevent you from making impulsive decisions and safeguard your profits. It can leverage your earnings and make sure you make much higher.

•The most important thing to bear in mind is that planning will teach you how important patience is. It is only through consistent patience that you will be able to attain your end goals.

Covered Call

Also known as a buy-write, this describes the act of selling the right to purchase a specified asset that you own at a specified price within a specified amount of time, which is usually less than 12 months. It is a two-part strategy whereby someone first purchases stock then sells it on the-share-by-share prices.

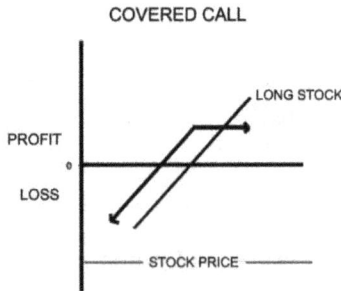

COVERED CALL

The beauty of this type of option is that the seller benefits by receiving a premium payment from the holder of the options. Risk is mitigated because the seller already owns the stock. Therefore, your costs are covered if the stock price rises above the strike price. If the trader chooses to exercise the right to purchase on or before the expiration date, you simply deliver as agreed and rip any additional benefits.

Stock is the most common asset used in this type of option.

If you choose to consider covered calls, at your price, you need to be willing to own the stock, and it is even if the price depreciates. Remember that there is no guarantee that you will earn significantly on the stock that you have purchased due to the volatility of financial markets. Therefore, you need to be diligent in your focus on seeking good quality stocks that you are willing to own. You need to be able to still potentially benefit from that ownership if there are down periods in the market.

As the seller of a covered call option, you need to be also willing to part with that stock if the price rises. You cannot change your mind if the price of the stock goes up if you have already entered into an option with a willing buyer. You must exercise that delivery if the trader chooses to use that option.

The maximum potential profit of covered calls will be achieved if the stock price is met at or above the strike price of that call at or by the expiration date. The formula for this is as follows:

- Sum of the Call Premium + (Strike Price - Stock Price) = Maximum Potential Profit

The seller also needs to consider the break-even point at the expiration date. The formula for this is as follows:

- Purchase Price of the Stock - The Call Premium = Break-Even Analysis

The seller also needs to determine the maximum risk potential. It is equal to the purchasing price of the stock at the break-even point.

The seller also needs to be satisfied with the static rate of return and the if-called rate of return on the stocks. The static performance is the approximate annual net profit of a covered call, assuming that the stock price does not change until the expiration date and until the option expires. To calculate this value, the seller needs to know:

- The purchase price of the particular stock
- The price of the option (strike)
- The price of the call
- The number of days until the option expires
- If there are any dividends and the amount of these dividends

Calculating these factors leads to a percentile figure being determined. The formula for calculating this is:

- (Call + Dividend) / Stock Price × Time Factor = Static Rate of Return

The if-called return is an approximate annual net profit on a covered call with the assumption that the stock price is above the strike price by or on the expiration of the option and that the stock is sold at termination. In calculating, the same factors need to be determined. The formula for calculating this is:

- (Call + Dividend) + (Strike - Stock Price) / Stock Price × Time Factor = If-Called Rate of Return

Iron Condor

If you think the price of a stock is going to stay within a specific range, you can sell to open an iron condor. This type of strategy requires you to buy a call and sell a call (creating a call credit spread), and buy a put and sell a put (creating a put credit spread). Let's see how it is built-in steps. All options in this strategy have the same expiration date.

IRON CONDOR

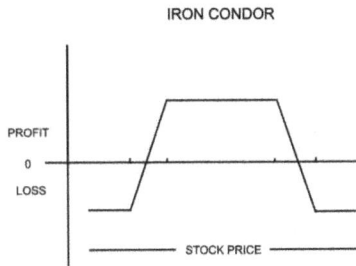

First, you pick an out-of-the-money call price, a bit above the current share price. You sell this call. Then you buy one with a strike that is a little higher. The net difference gives you credit.

Now you pick an out of the money put option that is below the current share price. Then you sell this put option. Next, you buy an out of the money put option that has an even lower strike price. The difference here gives you another credit.

The maximum profit is the net credits. The maximum loss is given by (width of strike prices)—entry price. The broker will make you put up enough cash to cover the loss unless you have a margin account.

The narrower you make your strike prices, the lower your maximum loss, but the higher the probability that you will experience a loss. The range is set by the two options you sell, and you want the stock price to stay within those bounds.

The iron condor is a great strategy to use for monthly income. It can work exceptionally well over short time frames, like a week, since that lessens the chance of the stock going outside the range. However, many traders use a month for their iron condors.

Iron Butterfly

An iron butterfly is another strategy to use if you think the stock price will stay within a specific range. It will use four options, like the iron condor, but there will be three different strike prices.

IRON BUTTERFLY

PROFIT

0

LOSS

———— STOCK PRICE ————

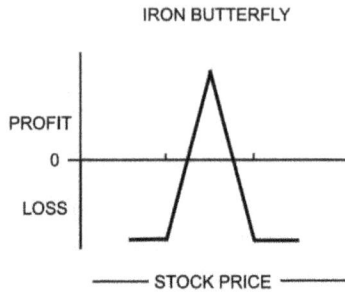

In this case, you will sell a put option and a call option with the same strike price. The strategy is to get as close to the money as possible. We will call the strike priced used the central strike. Then you set a differential price we will call x. Now you buy a put option with a strike price of (central strike − x), and you buy a call option with a strike price of (central strike + x).

Like an iron condor, the profit from an iron butterfly is fixed at the net credit when you sell to open. This is given by the sum of the premiums earned from selling the at the money call and put, minus the prices paid for the out of the money options.

The maximum loss is the strike price of the purchased call–strike price of the sold put–total premium.

Long Butterfly Strategy

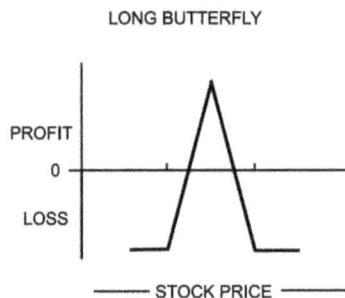

LONG BUTTERFLY

PROFIT

0

LOSS

———— STOCK PRICE ————

This strategy involves three parts where one put option is purchased at particular and then selling the other two options at a price lower than the buying price, and purchasing one put at an even lower price during a specific trading period.

Short Butterfly Strategy

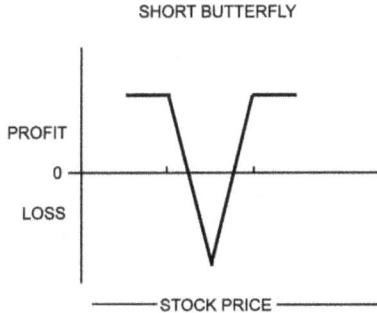

SHORT BUTTERFLY

PROFIT

0

LOSS

STOCK PRICE

In this strategy, three parts are still involved where a put option is sold at a much higher price, and two puts are then purchased at a lower price than the purchase price, and a put option is later on sold at a much lower strike price. In both cases, all put bear the same expiration date, and the strike prices usually are equidistant, as revealed in various options trading charts. A short butterfly strategy is the opposite way of a long butterfly strategy.

CONCLUSION

Thanks to the internet, the dream of financial freedom can be brought into reality much easier today. With an arrogant boss and a tiresome daily commute, there is no longer a need for all of us to put up with a less than stimulating job. There is the real potential to make a lot of money without ever having to set foot outside your own home as long as you understand how to use a computer and access a broadband connection.

Many people, through many online channels, have made it rich. If you are excited and interested in a particular kind of consumer item, such as clothing or video games, you may set up a website through which such products are sold. The significant aspect of being a network marketer is that your own home's items do not need to be stored. You collect customers' details and then pass them on to the shipper. You will be given a commission for each product you sell. There have been options trading, and a lot of people are trading in options.

First of all, financial freedom requires a strong residual source of income. How does one generate a residual source of income that is sufficient for financial freedom? You do that without having to work for it by producing reliable, consistent monthly revenue. So how can trading options help you accomplish that?

You first need a large fund that most beginners or individuals who simply want financial freedom do not have to start with to release residual income strong enough for financial freedom. This fact is where the leverage of options for trading comes in. Trading options give anyone with only a small amount of money a shot at quickly building a big fund through leveraged swing trading using a small fund. This trading will require a proven swing trading system, consistent and disciplined trading options, and good technical analysis skills. You will need to be able to determine the outlook on a stock or asset consistently and accurately and then select a strategy of options that is best designed to optimize the return on investment on such a move. It is possible to quickly multiply a small fund into something sizable when done correctly. And yes, it will not be easy, especially for the beginner, all the time, every time, to get such analysis and choice of options strategy right. As such, it is building a significant fund through the trading of options requires good education and guidance on options.

What you will accomplish from the book is a well-developed skill in trading options, and with its strategies, you will become a strong and successful trader of options.

www.ingramcontent.com/pod-product-compliance
Lightning Source LLC
Chambersburg PA
CBHW071500210326
41597CB00018B/2636